72 poems
John Robert Brown

Illustrations
Harry Venning

First published 2018 by IRON Press
5 Marden Terrace
Cullercoats
North Shields
NE30 4PD
tel +44(0)191 2531901
ironpress@xlnmail.com
www.ironpress.co.uk

ISBN 978-0-995-45-79-4-2
Printed by Imprint Digital

© The poems John Robert Brown 2018
© Artwork Harry Venning
© This collection IRON Press

Cover and book design Brian Grogan
Cover illustration Harry Venning

Typeset in Georgia 9pt

IRON Press books are distributed by
NBN International
and represented by Inpress Ltd
Churchill House, 12 Mosley Street,
Newcastle upon Tyne, NE1 1DE
tel: +44(0)191 2308104
www.inpressbooks.co.uk

John Robert Brown was born in 1941 and trained as an engineering draughtsman. Upon qualifying he abandoned his drawing office career to become a professional saxophonist and clarinettist, during which time he played in ship's orchestras, theatre pits, in the Hallé Orchestra, and in many BBC Radio broadcasts with his own small swing band, *John Brown's Bodies*.

He left full-time playing to read education at Nottingham University. After a brief spell teaching maths in a comprehensive school, he became a full-time lecturer on the pioneering jazz course at Leeds College of Music, where he directed ensembles and taught Harmony and the History of Jazz. During this period he was, for several years, chairman of the Clarinet and Saxophone Society of Great Britain.

Odd Socks is his first collection of verse.

Harry Venning is an award winning cartoonist, comedy writer and performer based in Brighton.

Harry's cartoons have appeared in publications as diverse as Mathematics Today, Radio Times, Music Teacher and The Stage. For twenty one years he has provided The Guardian with the weekly strip cartoon Clare In The Community, about an unaware and empathy-free social worker. In 2004 he developed Clare In The Community into a successful BBC Radio 4 sitcom currently on its twelfth series.

When not at a desk, Harry tours his cartoon workshop Release Your Inner Cartoonist around schools, theatres, arts centres and festivals.

As a youngster in prep school I was given a copy of *Alice in Wonderland*. I still possess that book, now foxed and battered, a hardback edition of war economy standard bearing an inscription written in my father's hand, dated 1948. The few poems of Lewis Carroll published therein, dated 1865, made a huge impression on me. Caroll's much-loved lines represent a weighty argument in favour of the chime of rhyme, the appeal of humour and the value of verse in the process of memorisation. Merely quote *"Will you walk a little faster?"* to any elderly well-read Englishman and he is likely to be able to fire back, word-perfect, the subsequent sentences of the *Mock Turtle's Song*.

My own developmental influences also include the charming end-rhymed couplets that accompanied the adventures of *Rupert Bear*, which I followed avidly day-by-day in *The Daily Express* newspaper throughout my childhood. Subsequently, because of my slightly-too-late teenage devotion to the great swing-era clarinettists Benny Goodman and Artie Shaw I was exposed to some of the beautifully crafted lyrics and melodies composed by Hoagy Carmichael, Johnny Mercer, Ira Gershwin, Cole Porter, Jerome Kern, Antônio Carlos Jobim and others. Then, in my adult years, I discovered entertaining verses by Edward Lear, W.S. Gilbert, Ogden Nash, John Betjeman, Philip Larkin, Wendy Cope, Pam Ayres and, recently, Brian Bilston - all grist to my comic verse mill. Among the satire and sagacity of these writers there is much I love and remember.

In preparing *Odd Socks* I am indebted to Peter Mortimer of Iron Press for taking on the project, and for putting much energy into seeing this small collection into print. When the talented Harry Venning agreed to contribute the cartoons, I was delighted.

I hope you enjoy the result.

John Robert Brown

The Poems

Testing, Testing.	9
Aitch	10
A Tip	11
Miss Cope's Profession	12
Railways	13
I am a College Principal	14
Foreign Language	15
A Cat Has To Check	16
Reading Allowed	17
Japanese Gyratory	18
Chanting	19
Eponyms	20
From the Gulf of Bothnia	21
In5ecurity	22
The Endoscope	23
Going Green	25
Marmalade	26
In The Barber's Window	27
Blemya	28
Taking the Cure	29
In The Bedroom	30
For Adolphe Sax	31
Writerly Habits	32
Aubade	33
Nothing Changes	34
Nuneaton	35
Deutsch im Englischen	36
Betty's Bettys	37
Rape of the Locks	38
Galoshes	40
Short Socks	41
Odd Socks	42
The Necktie	43
Button-Down Collar	44
Footwear at the Airport	45
Suits	46

Sole Music	47
A Beanie in Manhattan	48
Stripes on a Necktie	49
Questions from the Floor	50
Daylight Saving Time	51
The Miracle that is Grass	52
Prosopagnosia, or Face Blindness	53
Paracusis	54
The Tactless Child	55
Amateur Musicians	56
Speed	57
This Shower	58
Leonard Bernstein 1918-1990	59
Dipthongs	60
Where Next?	61
Ordination of Women	62
The Case	63
Doctor, Doctor	64
Alternative Facts	66
Tale from the Outback	67
Musée de bonnes chansons	68
Antipodean Reflections	69
For Alice?	70
That Mexican Wall	71
How Do I Get to Carnegie Hall?	72
Black and White	73
Russian Doll	74
Phalacrocorax	75
Saucer	76
Feline Help	77
Four-by-Four	78
Polysyllables	79
Pop Music	80
Somatotypes	81
Red Book	82
Things That Count	84

Testing, Testing.

Is this thing on?
    Don't blow upon
The mike. Certainly don't strike
    The thing to check how strong
It makes the sound. Don't pound!

Kindly tell that chap he mustn't tap.
    Can you hear me at the back?
No! NO! Please don't blow.
    Hello! HELLO!!
Three, four. One, TWO.

Mary had a little lamb,
    She also had a bear...
Okay - that'll do,
    One, two,
That'll be loud enough for you.

Aitch

The girl on the phone, from the HSBC,
   Says 'haitch' on the phone when speaking to me.
Perhaps aitch is something she's heard no one say?
   For she speaks of 'haitch' but aitch starts with A.'

A Tip

What do you gain by withholding a tip?
 My friend, you must meanness abjure.
Tipping your waitress will not make you broke,
 You hoarder, you skinflint, you bore.
What do you gain when no pour-boire you slip?
 You'll not be a popular bloke.
Twenty per cent is a generous drop,
 While half that will strike folk as tight.
Clearly de trop when, aged more than fifty,
 Good manners you constantly fight.
Such mean behaviour must come to a stop.
 Please, do not claim that you're thrifty.

Miss Cope's Profession

It says she began as an eacher.
   I confess I've assumed all along
That eacher must surely mean teacher.
   Eacher is teacher, spelt wrong.

This eacher appeared on the flyleaf
   Of her booklet of serious verse.
Her printer should really proof harder,
   His roof preading couldn't be worse.

Railways

If a Martian came to visit and travelled on our trains,
   I wonder, would he ask himself: "Do British folk lack brains?
Why not make the railway wider, broad gauge, like ours on Mars?
   If these Earthlings made these changes they'd need far fewer cars.
Why are British trains so short? Is the reason lack of thought?"

If a Martian went to Japan, where trains move fast as planes,
   He'd ask: "Why don't the Brits do that?" I wish I could explain
Just why our dining cars are closed and how our fares are planned.
   Or why our wretched commuters are forced each day to stand.
Why are British trains so sad? Martian man would think us mad.

I am a College Principal

I am a college principal. I have a PhD.
  I'm paid a handsome salary, I drive an SUV.
Music's what we're teaching here, from tuba to celeste.
  I wear a suit from Austin Reed; I hope I look well-dressed.

You ask me what it is I play. Well, these days I admit
  I chair the academic board, send down each thimblewit.
No, I don't play; I work from home, or hit the conference trail.
  But mostly I appoint new staff, and sign huge piles of mail.

I know about retention rates, and how consultants work,
  Can quote you aims, and mission statements, chastise staff who shirk,
Invest in People, validate, relax, take reading weeks,
  But can't adjust my marking with statistical techniques.

I write some minor papers (research is such a bore),
  Then fly abroad to read them out, to groups of three or four.
I specialise in arcane stuff, say free jazz, or brass bands,
  And have my travel subsidized by extra-mural grants.

You cannot hear me play, on disc or Radio Three.
  I don't write books and, sad to say, I'm never on TV.
Thus, few musicians know of me. Composing's not my sphere.
  Despite all this I claim an international career.

I am a college principal. I have a PhD.
  I'm paid a handsome salary, and drive an SUV.

Foreign Language

Yankee folk use words of their own,
   Of a vayse or of 'erbs they speak.
Their bottom they call a fanny,
   A word that to Brits sounds comique.

Decatur chimes with equator,
   Poughkeepsie with gipsy will rhyme.
Nu-cu-lar bomb is hopelessly wrong,
   And aloominum and Eye-raq are such truly awful mispronunciations that to use them should certainly be categorised as a petty crime.

A Cat has to Check

Non-stop the rain fell this morning.
  Minna stood by the back door,
Watching the rain for long minutes,
  Then looked from the front, to be sure.

Reading Allowed

Words that share sounds are a challenge to writers,
  In verses, may one recite them?
Are readers allowed to say them aloud?
  Pray, give me an instance, this instant.

Does it make sense to pay cents for cheap scents?
  Do canons, or cannons, have balls?
Could one use yews to fence in one's ewes?
  One shouldn't rouse rows should one do so.

Would builders dare alter an altar
  By the aisle of the church on the isle?
Words that share sounds are a challenge to writers,
  Please, say them aloud, it's allowed.

Japanese Gyratory
(Roundabouts arrive in Japan, 2013)

In Japan, and new this year,
  Traffic roundabouts appear.

Mazdas, Hondas now gyrate,
  Drivers must negotiate

Clockwise circles. We'll survive,
  Glad I didn't choose to drive.

Hooters silent, all polite.
  Taxi drivers' gloves are white,

Driving on the left we go,
  Grateful that the traffic's slow.

Should he filter? He's no clue.
  Mind that Lexus! "After you."

Can't browse signs; could go astray,
  Though white arrows point our way.

Nevertheless, I feel absurd
  - I can't read a single word.

Japan's taxis painted green,
  Highly-polished limousine.

Driver's masked, no-one gets ill.
  Never tip, just pay the bill.

Drivers sit. Somehow, they bow;
  Roundabouts in Japan now.

Chanting

Seven eights are fifty-six;
    Chant your tables every day,
Speak the answer, 'til it sticks;
    Doing sums will seem like play.

Six times nine are fifty-four.
    Chant your tables, daily task.
This your class all know, I'm sure,
    Any multiple - just ask.

Five times five make twenty-five,
    'Times five' ends in five, or nought.
Answers simple to derive,
    Chants in fives take little thought;

Four times twelve are forty-eight,
    Learn to multiply by rote.
Say it fast, don't hesitate.
    That's the way that wins my vote.

Learn by heart to own this stuff,
    How else to learn? Who's to say?
I know, I know. Yes, yes, it's tough,
    But slapdash sums will earn poor pay.

Eponyms

Léon Theremin
   Is the eponym
Of the Theremin.*
   For an eponym
Is merely a thing
   After which something
Is named. Think of its
   Etymology,
Or of Louis Braille
   And his Braille System.

It means 'giving name'.
   Like Biro, or Colt,
Or Geiger, or Ford,
   Or Ampère, or Volt,
The Marquis de Sade,
   Or Rolls, Royce and Ritz
And dear Granny Smith.
   It's simply a thing,
After which something
   Is named.
        As I've explained.

An early electronic musical instrument.

From the Gulf of Bothnia

Sitting in port in St Petersburg
  I decided to jot down some lines.
Would it be perverse if terse Bothnian verse
  Held rouble entendre, or worse?

In5ecurity

A number m4ke5 your pa55word more effect!ve
 But, neverthe£e55, it cou£d be cr4cked by a detect!ve.
Wor5e, when he4rd, thi5 ver5e i5 defect!ve.

It'5 po55ible you'll feel absurd
 If the c£everne55 of your new pa55word
Mu5t for all t!me rem4in unhe4rd.

The Endoscope

She holds my arm, slips on the cuff,
  Then gives the rubber bulb a puff.
Left arm is squeezed. A little wait.
  Nurse reads out: 'B. P.: one-one-eight.'

Next I see the phlebotomist,
  Who smiles and bids me: 'Clench your fist.
Just a scratch,' said matter-of-fact.
  In truth, the scratch is worse than that.

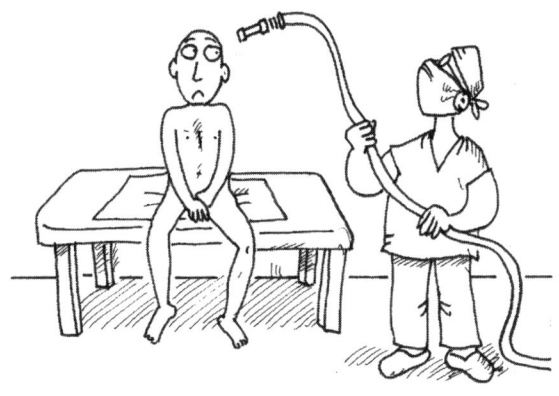

Most dire with which I've had to cope,
  The entry of an endoscope.
My penis is the chosen route.
  Discomfort caused? Great, most acute.

Camera mounted on a stick
  To give a view in, up my dick.
'You care to look?' The surgeon asks.
  I wince, but watch this complex task.

Urethra's bore is very thin,
  It's not evolved to let things in.
Not anyone's idea of fun,
  Such actions made my old eyes run.

Adversity of the Third Age?
  Against these hurts one should not rage.
These trials through which we choose to live
  Surpass the grim alternative.

Going Green

She owns a lawn of emerald green,
   Which cost a massive price.
It gleams with a sheen that's seldom seen,
   Men came to fit it, twice.

No birds search here for grub or fly,
  No butterflies here hover.
No mower needs she now to buy
  - A plastic lawn's no bother.

Marmalade

Jams and jellies in abundance at that New York breakfast bar.
    Yet no marmalade is proffered.
How can this be? *Je ne sais quoi.*

Bitter flavour, dark and chunky, sticky treat we Brits applaud
    Our daily choice when we're at home;
No tasty marjam when abroad.

Does bitterness put people off? Surely not, it tastes so nice.
    Such a pity, what they're missing.
Pack your own is my advice.

In the Barber's Window

A creature, stuffed, and on display
   Prompts the question: 'Why is that so?'
And where's the pole of red and white?
   Don't ask me. Please, how would I know?
Why is a rabbit here on show?
   Oh - I see.
      It's a *hare!*
      Ho-ho.

Blemya

A shrunken form, of neck devoid,
  His eyes and mouth are on his chest.
Strange fierce Blemya has no head and
  I've heard some say he'd eat a guest.

He's flat of face, and flat of lips,
  With small round holes instead of eyes.
An ugly trunk, no head, no neck,
  He's said to bake his foes in pies!

Where to view a Blemya's likeness?
  Carved in wood, man-eating creature,
If his form you wish to gaze on
  There's one in Ripon cannot eat yah.

Ripon Cathedral, in North Yorkshire, has a set of medieval misericords which includes a woodcarving of the mythical Blemya.

Taking the Cure

In Harrogate, you really oughter
   Sip a glass of local water.
Though some tastes nice,
   (It's good with ice),
I must confess
   I feel distress,
And can't address
   A drink which tastes of H.S.

In the Bedroom

Morning. Dozing in my room,
   No sound, no word, is said.
Softly Kate creeps through the gloom.
   To crawl into my bed.
Lovely female snuggles near.
   Downstairs, my wife: "You-hoo?"
Kate pretends she cannot hear.
   "Darling… is Kate Cat with you?"

For Adolphe Sax

Don't ever call a saxophone a sax,
    A terse abbreviation, lacking style.
A sousaphone is never called a sue,
    You wouldn't call a xylophone a xyle.

You'll never hear a saxhorn called a sax,
    By doing so you'd certainly mislead.
A saxhorn is a different kind of sound,
    A member of the brass, another breed.

No, please don't call a saxophone a sax,
    Lest people think you're slightly lower class.
Sax was a famous Belgian, not a pipe.
    A person, not a tube of polished brass.

Writerly Habits

Check each book index; see if you're there,
  Constantly google your name.
Your book to the front on the bookshelves,
  Promote only you, without shame.

Then scan each day's paper for obits.
  When did your rival depart?
Ignore what he wrote in his lifetime,
  Thank God! You outlived the old fart.

Aubade

Early morning coos a dove,
   Pianissimo and distant.
First sound I hear, so quiet, so clear,
   Gentle, but insistent.

The cat claws at the bedroom door,
   Asking to be fed.
Then milkman clinks his burdened crate,
   Soon time to face the day ahead.

Is sleep done? I yawn; methinks
   I'll take another forty winks.
Then: Clatter! Bang! Sharp hiss of brake,
   Wow! Now, for sure, I'm wide awake.

Oh dear. Get up! It's my mistake,
   Today the bin men call.

Nothing Changes

When first discussed, they called it Jass.
    Soon, posters spelled it Jazz.
They changed the name because small boys
    Defaced the word to 'ass'.

Nuneaton

One could write many words about Nuneaton,
  The largest town in Warwickshire today,
How sad though now to know
  While coal earned Nunny's dough,
Black lung took many miners' lives away.

Nobody ever writes about Nuneaton,
  A Midlands town most visitors find dull.
No moonlight over Bond Gate,
  Or strolls round Arbury Estate,
Can ever tempt the poet to extol.

Nobody ever writes about Nuneaton.
  No novels ever use her in their plot.
George Eliot called her *Milby*.
  Those who seek to name her will be
Advised that here's a town that isn't hot.

Nobody ever writes about Nuneaton.
  Scribes tend to leave the little town alone.
Few people give a hoot
  For Pool Bank Street or Long Shoot,
Nuneaton's charms are doomed to stay unknown.

Deutsch im Englischen

Sauerkraut and *Dachshund* are good German words,
  And *Rucksack* and *Zeitgeist* I'd list
As words filched by Brits, because there's no match;
  That's why we use *kaputt* and *Kitsch*.

We all speak of *Strudel*, *Gestalt* and *Wurst*,
  Though Hamburger some mistranslate.
Yet Brits lack a word to mean *Treppenwitz*
  - A quip thought up moments too late.

Kindergarten we find very useful,
  Like *Angst* or *Ersatz*, I suggest.
But please let's develop our fine native words
  In Britain, in English should I not be addressed?

Betty's Bettys

It feels wrong, seeing 'Bettys' thus.
  I hesitate to make a fuss,
But 'Betty's' is how it should be.
  Yet Bettys (no apostrophe)
Is, alas, what customers see...
  Ignore the grammar; pour the tea!

But if this verse is read to you,
  My point is lost. What can I do?

Rape of the Locks

Ron chose to be a barber,
   Styling hair his one desire.
With his skill his till he'd fill,
   First, a name must Ron acquire.

Starting out with *Making Waves*,
   Ali Barber seemed quite neat,
Miss Tress sounded good (for girls),
   Could Ron trade as *On Mane Street*?

Some thought his wordplay witty,
   And his puns his own reword.
'Barberism' sneered others,
   Who thought Ron's names absurd.

Barber Black Sheep caused a groan,
   Julius Scissor? Would that date?
At *Jack the Clipper* readers winced
   - While *His and Hairs* they didn't rate.

Dare he try *Curl Up and Dye*?
   Would folk moan at *Shearlock's Home*?
Ron's puns were mostly awful,
   - Including *Hair O' Dome*.

Now Ron owns that barber's shop,
   Stylish customers are groomed.
Ron is skilled, his till is filled,
   And his business has boomed.

You ask did Ron quit punning.
  If you visit him these days
His shop's called *Crops and Bobbers*,
  So, no, Ron hasn't changed his ways.

Galoshes

Galoshes slip over your shoes
  To keep out the sludge and the wet.
They're really rubberised slippers
  To render bad weather no threat.

Now démodé, along with lorgnettes,
  Straw boaters, plus-fours, or men's cloaks.
But, my dear friend, don't deride them,
  Ignore cheeky folks who make jokes.

Galoshes - uncommon, but useful,
  I'm sorry they're viewed as passé.
When facing deep slush in my loafers,
  For galoshes, I say hooray!

Short Socks

His socks too short,
  His legs so white.
Crossed legs reveal
  An ugly sight.

Odd Socks

*Professor Richard Dawkins, the atheist,
sometimes wore odd socks on television.*

Richard Dawkins, when on TV,
   Sometimes wears socks that don't agree.
His left sock's red, his right sock's green,
   A sight like this is seldom seen.
Expect surprise or daring views
   When speakers' socks have different hues.

Professor Dawkins, smartly dressed,
   Has the clergy most distressed.
He's the man whose big conclusion
   Says: 'God is Merely Man's Delusion'.
God-fearing types, expect a catch
   When your speaker's socks don't match.

The Necktie

"You should have worn your tie," she said,
    Who'd have me wear the thing in bed.
"It hides your sagging neck from view,
    Listen to what I say to you."

I disagree.

Away with silken semaphore!
  My fancy ties I'll wear no more.
Few men are donning them today.
  From public life, they've slipped away.

Men's neckties, once the latest hots,
  These days no more than dated knots.

Button-Down Collar

American style, worn to prevent
  Collar points flapping.
Button-down charm
  Goes with a jacket - the single-vent.

Undo that tie! Choose a brown loafer.
  Off with that suit!
Better a blazer.
    Heed what I say, Sir:
        Bold nonchalance is what one should go fer.

Footwear at the Airport

Contemplating x-ray queues
Slip-on shoes are what I choose
    At the check-in, when I'm seeking time to gain.

Speedily I'm in my socks,
Shoeless, fast, unorthodox,
    When checking-in for travelling on a plane.

Suits

His several gaudy bespoke suits
   Were garments that he treasured.

He declared: "I'll never ever wear them
   But I just love being measured."

Sole Music

Through the sole of my shoe, I think there's a nail.
   It's one of a pair I bought in a sale.
(That's the nail, not the shoe, about which I complain).
   I walk on my heels, from the pain.

Through the sole of my shoe? It could be a tack.
   I wobble, I can't keep on track.
I need a good cobbler's legerdemain
   As the forecast now warns me of rain.

Through the sole of my shoe there's a spike,
   As my brogue is now leaking, I yearn for my bike.
I'll be wearing wet socks; I'll catch the flu.
   What shall I do? I'll be going ahh-choo.
Due, yes, it's true, to that nail in my shoe.

A Beanie in Manhattan

He was wearing a watch cap, in wool, coloured black.
    White letters spelled 'NY', I asked: "What is that?
What does NY mean? North Yorkshire, perhaps?"
    "New York," he growled, adding: "Man, don't be a prat."

Stripes on a Necktie

The necktie is falling from favour,
    I'm sorry to see such a trend.
I won't lie; I am shy, saying 'bye to my tie,
    For it tells where I come from, my friend.

Geography dictates a difference of style,
    And how a man's tie is designed.
I'm thinking of stripes, the diagonal sort,
    And have mostly Americans in mind.

In Europe, tie stripes point from heart down to hand
    Going from left down to right,
But 'Merican stripes cross the opposite way
    - If in doubt, well, consult a website.

I can tell you, the reasons are many
    And go a long way back, you will find.
About this, some men have penned essays;
    How sublime, had I time
        To explain it in rhyme.

Questions from the Floor

There's many a time I want to yell
   At those who don't know 'ask' from 'tell'.
Of a statement posed as a query
   I've become extremely weary.
How can a speaker remain civil
   Answering ego-centred drivel?
Dull ramblings from a deadly bore
   Should be declared against the law.
Such pronouncements, expressed at length,
   Set off the thought: 'God, give me strength.'
Know that when you stand to ask a question,
   Brevity gives the best impression.

Daylight Saving Time

In late March we *spring* our clocks forward;
 Then have them *fall* back in the fall.
Changing the clocks dispenses a shock,
  When dusk comes in no time at all.

The light was much brighter this morning,
 Though I spent one hour less in bed.
Such pantomime, this shifting of time.
 Why not alter our conduct, instead?

This shift was begun by the Germans
 Striving to win the Great War.
Though, to save cash spent on candles,
  Some considered the plan long before.

Today there are seventy countries
 Whose clocks alter twice every year.
Arizona's the loner; clocks there don't change.
 How wise! Could we not try that here?

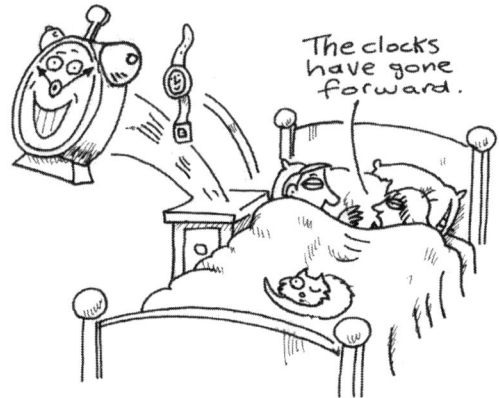

The Miracle that is Grass

The horse feeds on grass, gallops out in the sun,
  Drinks only water, is inexpensive to run.
Though lambs look quite different, they eat the same food
  As geese, llamas, and cattle. What can one conclude?

Prosopagnosia, or Face Blindness

Prosopagnosia is a disorder of mind,
    Where you might fetch the wrong child from school.
'Face Blindness' has these days this weird word defined.
    How alarming, one would feel such a fool
Giving gushing 'hellos' to strangers you meet,
    Or maybe pushing your wife out of bed,
Or snubbing that neighbour you pass in the street,
    Such despicable deeds you would dolefully dread.
Should all of your friends suffer prosopagnosia,
    You'd be certain to find that nobody knowsia.

Paracusis

"That lion has a lovely name," was what I thought she said.
   How could she know his moniker? Perhaps something she'd read?
"Tell me, what *is* he called?" I asked, by way of a reply.
   "It's mane, not name," she then explained, and smiled a jaded sigh.

I'm not exactly deaf. However, talk comes blurred these days.
   Between a sound and what it means exists a sonic haze.
I hear of 'Soviet Jewellery', catch chat of 'cute-eye strain',
   And one friend tells of dreadful smells close by a 'clogged-up train'.

The word which now describes my state (where meaning is capsized,
   And I hear that Ornette Coleman won a large 'Pullet Surprise')
Is paracusis, as when James heard that he must wash his knees,
   When all that had been requested was that Jim should watch his niece.

The Tactless Child

Too early to the terminus
 They'd come to catch the waiting bus.

Upstairs, the seats were slats of wood.
 The youngster didn't sit, but stood

To face a woman sat behind,
 Whose hirsute chin engaged his mind.

What happened next made Mother wince,
 Though young 'un didn't even flinch.

Loudly, youngster asked his question
 Spoken bold, without discretion,

The bus so silent all could hear:
 "Has she a beard from drinking beer?"

Amateur Musicians

A professor I know strums the banjo
  When he sings at the pub, in the bar.
Far worse is the medic
  Who gives me a headick
When he plays his electric guitar.

Would anyone swoon at the croaking bassoon
  Of that lady who drives a Mercedes?
She works in an office,
  Plays bassoon like a novice,
And her playing evokes thoughts of Hades.

And as for that oboe-ing farmer,
  Whose tone could well curdle fresh milk,
If he'd chosen to pick
  The liquorice stick
He still wouldn't be Acker Bilk.

Speed

Late for the funeral
    He drove without heed for fate.
Took two too many chances;
    Now he, too, is late.

This Shower

This shower won't do what I require,
    Runs cold, then hot. Why, I enquire?
The heat so great that I perspire;
    Too, too hot.

Controls have me in a flap,
    Which way do I turn the tap?
A puzzle for this parboiled chap,
    In a spot.

Each hotel room, different plumbing,
    First, one scalds. Next, cold that's numbing.
Shower taps suffer this shortcoming:
    Fry or freeze.

Compel all plumbers: standardise!
    Protect us from a wet surprise.
Till then, immersion satisfies.
    Bath? Yes, please!

Leonard Bernstein, 1918-1990

'Leave Him Not, by G.H.Swinger'
   - An anagram by Lennie B.
'The Man I Love', by George (J.) Gershwin,
   That's where it comes from, not from me.

'An Orchestra Is Not a Carthorse',
   Also came from Mr Bernstein.
'Be Silent, Listen', he would say,
   Yes, that's another Lenny line.

Conductor, pianist, teacher, too;
   A member of my own Top Ten.
Remembered best for *West Side Story*,
   We'll never see his like again.

Composed *Mass*, and *On the Town*,
   And an anagram that makes me glum.
Have you heard it? So ironic:
   'Funeral' becomes 'Real Fun'.

Dipthongs

The Germans have a clever way
   Their Deutsche double vowels to say.
Two vowels when paired, like E and I,
   (Dipthongs, let me clarify),
In Deutschland, stress the second vowel;
   If put the other way, they'll howl.

Thus: *Bernstein*, please, in talk of Lenny,
   Never, ever, 'Bernsteen'. Many
Americans still say it thus,
   But if you hear them, make a fuss.
If you hear a mangled dipthong,
   Inform them that they got it wrong.

Where Next?

At the end of your vocation,
   No longer tied by occupation,
Will you think of relocation,
     When you retire?

Will you live beside the sea,
   Maybe dwell there *en famille*?
Or settle in a new country,
     May I enquire?

Will life be one long holiday,
   Will you live the life soigné
And end up dwelling far away,
     For many years?

Are there hobbies you'll pursue,
   Other things you'll want to do,
Maybe visit Uluru,
     Or home-brew beers?

Perhaps you'll curse the day you stirred,
   Feel that both of you have erred,
Regard your state as most absurd;
     Are you upset?

Now you've concluded your vocation,
   Brought to an end your occupation,
Tell me, is your new location
     Cause for regret?

Ordination of Women

Attractive Wendy, pious lady,
   Was consecrated priest today.
Does that mean that Holy Wendy
   Can now be termed a Bird of Pray?

The Case

This strong wooden case
    Is the quiet, secret, place
Where, these days, my staunch old friend quietly abides.

This friend shared my life
    For years. Yes, pre-wife;
Now this case is the place where my pal always hides.

Now he's not heard much,
    But still keeps his touch,
And those rare occasions you'll never forget.

You've not heard him yet?
    Dear, have you not met?
Here, in blackwood and silver, greet my fine clarinet.

Doctor, Doctor

Joe Scram, BSc, had a good first degree,
    But never enrolled for a PhD.
An advert that offered PhDs for sale
    He spotted, I think, in the *Hull Daily Mail*.
Scram sent off a cheque (but no dissertation)
    By return he received his fake qualification.

Scram carried on teaching, received his award,
    And was appointed onto Academic Board.
Joe Scram was hoping to earn extra pay,
    And felt no disgrace at behaving this way.
Now, known to all as Doctor Joe Scram,
    It was then that sham Scram got himself in a jam.

For Scram had cards printed, with the title 'Professor',
    Then grabbed free-lance work as a college assessor.
He wasn't a prof, his was purely a pose:
    - A real academic would look down his nose
At Scram, with his doctorate not worth a damn.
    Then, Joe encountered the man to block Scram.

It was when our chum Scram, in an oral exam,
    Expounded on rhyme schemes in *Omar Khayyám*.
Scram bluffed about meter, slant-rhymes and stanzas,
    His answer would equal two extravaganzas!
But hearing his sophistry, in that very same hall
    Was just the right person Joe Scram's bluff to call.

This colleague, Bill Oak, now took Scram to task,
    He'd read English at Oxford; Bill knew what to ask.
He talked about simile, a dactyl or two,
    And, concerning melisma, Bill Oak had a view,
He spoke of spondee and trochee - he was very well-read -
    Talked of cadence, chiasmus, 'til Scram's ears well-nigh bled!

Such withering derision delivered by Oak
    With stylish concision, was clearly no joke.
Oak cited caesura, ballad, closed form,
    Scram was now quaking. Oh, what a storm!
On 'point of view', Oak's tirade truly flowed,
    In reproving his victim, Oak could really unload.

The trembling Scram, now exposed as a sham,
    Tossed his doctorate as far as any man can.
I must say, in fairness, that Scram was quite bold,
    His confessing to cheating a thing to behold.
But, please, if you see PhDs up for sale,
    I hope you'll not buy. Do remember Scram's tale.

Alternative Facts

Remember the name of Sean Spicer*,
   A spokesman a tad inexact.
His lies are not lies, so he tells all the guys,
   But merely alternative facts.

If truth is defined by the White House,
   And reporters can all be denied,
Then Spicer's black's white, D.J.T.'s always right,
   Though we know Trump can speak from his backside.

How to deal with the well-meaning Spicer,
   Whose behaviour comes as a surprise?
Ignore any briefing you have no belief in,
   For Alternative Facts are mere lies.

In 2017 the personable White House press secretary Sean Spicer annoyed members of the the news media by reading a prepared statement in which he accused the press of minimizing impressions of President Donald J.Trump's crowd sizes.

Tale from the Outback

He talked lots of sand plains and salt pans,
    That make up so much of Down Under.
As this was his second language,
    Sometimes, we were all left to wonder.

From Melbourne he went down to Geelong,
    To ride his horse out and about.
He lost his way, then phoned up to say:
    "My steed ran off into the backout."

Musée de bonnes chansons

About songwriting they were sometimes wrong,
    The broadcasters; how ill they understood
What was bad or good.
    In Blackburn and Suessdorf's *Moonlight in Vermont*, for instance,
Just another song when first heard in '44,
    The length is a rare 28 bars.
The lyrics form a Haiku, 5-7-5; they don't rhyme.
    Something delightful falls on our ears, I suggest.
Now this terrific song is all-but forgotten, as time
    Moves steadily on, yes, like ski trails on a mountainside.
The well-spoken broadcaster scratches his fat rump in the studio,
    And continues to torture us, with enthusiasm rather than expertise.

Antipodean Reflections

Mark departs for New Zealand from Heathrow, at dawn.
On such a long flight he could feel quite forlorn.
And in less than two days he'll be in Wellington town,
Back with the Kiwis, all upside down.

For Mark Donlon in Wellington.

For Alice?

There's Michael, at the piano,
   On the ground floor of the store.
Smartly he's dressed,
   Jacket well-pressed,
His smile's a mile wide as he comes through the door.

For thirty-two years Mike has played here,
   His Steinway heard five days a week.
He'll never protest
   At the tunes you request,
Each day Mike will play all the tunes that you seek.

Sometimes a shopper pronounces words wrong
   Yet, if that happens, they might still hear their song.
In response without malice,
   Wise Mike, never callous,
Will deduce *Für Elise* from requests 'For Alice'.

   For Michael Hope in Sydney.

That Mexican Wall

We know that most walls fail, or fall.
   From 'sixty-one, East Berlin City
Was focus of much Allied pity.
   Donald Trump, please don't build that wall.

Great Wall of China, earth's famous
   Wall. Built to maintain Mongols at bay,
A long-term failure; Today I pray:
   Donald Trump, oh please don't shame us.

Hadrian's Wall, not quite as long,
   A Brit defence to Scots invasion,
Who easily performed evasion.
   Donald Trump, such walls are wrong.

How do I get to Carnegie Hall?

Concerning practice, Jack did what they say:
   "Play studies and scales for four hours a day."
I'm delighted to say (hip-hip-hooray)
   At Carnegie Hall Jack was then booked to play.

Jack thought this would be the gig of his life.
   Oh, what disappointment! What trouble! What strife!
When Jack revealed, to his doting wife,
   That *his* Carnegie Hall's in Dumfermline, Fife.

Black-and-White

See a magpie, or an orca,
  Keys, on Chopin's piano in Majorca
    - in black-and-white, all gleaming bright.

That youth, in co-respondent shoes,
  Or panda, biting buds off new bamboos
    - they, too, look right in black-and-white.

An ermine, in the winter,
  Or a skunk, that tiny two-tone stinker
    - in fur of black-and-white, stand out.

A Friesian cow, an albino rat,
  A bibbed and spatted old tuxedo cat
    - such pelts give great delight, no doubt.

Sharp peaks by Ansel Adams, bold
  uncommon pictures, we love to behold
    - stark monochrome crests by moonlight.

Silent movies, back in the day,
  Brave black headlines in USA Today;
    Yes, see them clear, in black and white.

Russian Doll

A superb nesting doll, a Soviet Matryoshka,
    Was prepared for the eminent Oskar Kokoshka.
There, inside Kokoshka's pristine Matryoshka,
    Lurked three shrinking versions…of Oskar Kokoshka.

Phalacrocorax

The cormorant perches by the lake
   Her wings spread wide for drying.
I wonder why she doesn't try
   To dry wet wings by flying?

Saucer

Whenever anything warm I sup,
   I spurn a mug or plastic cup.
That's not because I strike a pose
   (I do not have a toffee-nose).
My saucer catches every drip
   Falling from the cup I sip.
Also, I find it's such a boon
   To have a place to put my spoon.

Feline Help

Early at my desk today
   I can't begin; cat's in the way.
Sitting there, to purr and preen,
   My cat's so fat she blocks the screen.
If I ever feel like shirking,
   My portly cat helps stop me working.

Four-by-Four

Large and lavish vehicle, built in Solihull,
    Said to conquer any landscape or terrain.
In your superb four-by-four,
    Equipped to tackle every chore,
Why ride wide around that little kerbside drain?

Polysyllables

Did you hear about poor Doreen Barratt,
    That lady who owned a fine red-and-green parrot?
She lived in a garret, fed her parrot fresh carrot,
    And then she took a turn for the worse after being unable to finish due to a perverse dearth of verse, eventually giving up, but only after Doreen Barratt became quite desparrot.

Pop Music

She says 'Jazzy-Pop' is the music she croons.
              Perhaps *Tizer Rag* describes one of her tunes?

Somatotypes

Does an ectomorph live an 'ectic life?
   Is that why he looks so thin?
If he ate all day, would the same he weigh,
   Never to spring a double-chin?

Does an endomorph look as though he's scoffed,
   Like a hog from a brim-full trough?
Is this a cat too fat, a greedy brat,
   Who can never gobble enough?

Better choose to stay on the middle way
   Of the mesomorphs, the mean.
Choose regulation, strict moderation,
   Be neither larded nor lean.

Red Book

I'm amused to contemplate
   Recreations of the great.
Should this game appeal to you
   The details are in *Who's Who?*

It's an oversize red book
   Which gives me pleasure to look
At what is listed within
   - And the facts are genuine.

One Lord plays his Gretsch guitars,
   Several claim to study stars.
Drawing, travel, music, sport,
   Pastimes shown of every sort.

Wine and loafing, time to dream,
   Apophthegms, aspects of steam,
Writing poems, rural life,
   Even walking with one's wife!

I see - and here do not deride me -
   One toils to keep his office tidy.
Some good and great are comic actors,
   You'll find here several benefactors.

One of our famous MBEs
   Passes time devouring cheese.
Another spends his time by thinking;
   Could 'study of wine' be code for drinking?

Writing poems, eating well,
    One flies a chopper (made by Bell).
Playing trombone, trips to Venice,
    Making jam, or playing tennis

You'll be amused to contemplate
    The recreations of the great.
Should this game appeal to you
    The relevant facts are in *Who's Who?*

Things that Count

Two is good company, three is a crowd,
  While four, when three are guitars,
Can play very loud. By loud I mean forte,
   That's *forte*, not forty.
Oh, careless of me, I'm getting in front
   - As can four musicians, if I may be blunt.

Five is a side, or five fingers each hand,
  Six is a cricket drive, over the stand.
At sixes and sevens you're truly at sea,
  While ate is what happened to yesterday's tea.
Nine sounds like a German when he's saying no
  Please, don't interrupt! Don't stop my flow.

Next, to reject any trend to economy,
   Printed just twice, once in Deuteronomy,
Printed just twice, once in Deuteronomy,
   The old Ten Commandments, find them in the Bible.
Then, right behind ten (it's entirely reli'ble)
   Comes Apollo Eleven, first men on the Moon.

Twelve make a jury, all good men and true,
  Thirteen is unlucky. Why? I have not a clue.
Don't blur fourteen with forty, lest people will mock,
  Note: fourteen means two on the military clock.
Fifteen is a team that plays rugby football,
  And with that, I am finished.
               I mean it.
                   That's all.

IRON Press is among the country's longest
established independent literary publishers.
The press began operations in 1973 with IRON
Magazine which ran for 83 editions until 1997.
Since 1975 we have also brought out a regular list of
individual collections of poetry, fiction and drama
plus various anthologies ranging from *The Poetry of
Perestroika*, through *Limerick Nation,
100 Island Poems* and *Cold Iron, Ghost Stories
from the 21st Century.*

The press is one of the leading independent
publishers of haiku in the UK.
Since 2013 we have also run a regular IRON Press
Festival round the harbour in our native Cullercoats.
IRON in the Soul, our third festival,
took place in Summer 2017 a fourth festival
is planned for 2019.

We are delighted to be a part of
Inpress Ltd, which was set up by Arts Council
England to support independent literary publishers.
Go to our website (www.ironpress.co.uk)
for full details of our titles and activities.